For my friend, Peggy Thomas

Published in 2004 by The Rosen Publishing Group, Inc.
29 East 21st Street, New York, NY 10010

First Edition

Editor: Frances E. Ruffin
Book Design: Emily Muschinske

Photo Credits: Cover and title page (right), p. 16 © Independence National Historic Park; cover and title page (left), p. 4 © The Mariner's Museum, Newport News, Virginia; pp. 7, 8, 12, 15, 20 © North Wind Picture Archives; p. 11 © Dover Publications; p. 19 © Stock Montage/SuperStock.

Krebs, Laurie.
A day in the life of a colonial shipwright / by Laurie Krebs.— 1st ed.
    p. cm. — (The library of living and working in colonial times)
Includes bibliographical references (p.   ) and index.
  ISBN 0-8239-6227-X (library binding)
1. Shipwrights—United States—Juvenile literature. 2. United States—History—Colonial period, ca. 1600–1775—Juvenile literature. [1. Shipwrights. 2. United States—Social life and customs—To 1775.] I. Title. II. Series.
  HD8039.S52 U55 2003
  623.8'44'02373—dc21

                                                        2001005471

Manufactured in the United States of America

John Langdon was a colonial sea captain and shipwright who existed in the 1700s. Some of America's first warships were built in Langdon's shipyard in Portsmouth, New Hampshire. John Paul Jones and his ship, the *Ranger*, also existed. The character of Benjamin Tuthill and the events surrounding the launching of the *Ranger* are fictionalized. The descriptions of shipbuilding are factual.

Contents

Shipwright Apprentice

On a hot summer morning in 1777, Benjamin Tuthill crossed the bridge from Portsmouth, New Hampshire, to Badger Island. He entered Langdon Shipyard, dropped his tool sack, and wiped his forehead. Ben didn't notice the heat. He was too excited. Today the yard was **launching** the *Ranger*, the **sloop of war** he had helped to build. In 1776, when he turned sixteen, Ben began an **apprenticeship** with the shipwright, or shipbuilder, John Langdon. He had been working on the *Ranger* ever since.

A colonial shipyard was a busy place.

Langdon Shipyard

Ben saw Mr. Langdon and waved. As owner and master shipwright of the yard, John Langdon had designed the *Ranger*. From his drawings he first made a **scale model**, then drew life-size patterns of the ship.

Groups of men known as saw gangs were sent to cut down oak and pine trees that matched the drawing's measurements. In summer and fall, Ben helped to cut and to saw the wood to the pattern's size. By January the workers moved into the mold loft, a huge shed where the ship would be built.

This is a woodcut of a New England shipyard. ▶

Building the Skeleton

In the eighteenth century, it took from 20 to 30 craftsmen to build a wooden ship. Ships were made by hand. The craftsmen were Ben's teachers. As they laid the **keel**, or the ship's backbone, Ben learned to scarf, which is to join two pieces of wood together to make a beam the exact length of the keel. Ben attached wooden supports into the *Ranger*'s frame. He fit a curved piece to the center of the ship's **bow** and a straight post at the ship's rear, or stern. Then he fastened **ribs** to the keel to shape the **hull's** graceful lines.

◀ *A shipwright had to learn all the skills needed to build a ship.*

The Inside Story

Once the *Ranger*'s framework was completed, Ben covered the outside with oak boards called planks. The planks were soaked in hot water to make them damp and bendable. Then they were fastened to the frame with wooden pegs called trunnels.

Long, flat boards, called shelves, were bolted to the frame to hold the beams that ran across the width of the ship. Ben laid planks on the shelves for the *Ranger*'s deck. The work bruised his knees and scarred his hands.

This man is hammering wooden pegs into a ship's planking. ▶

A Seal of Approval

This morning, **caulkers** were checking the *Ranger*'s hull for open spaces between the planks. Ben reached into his sack for his caulking iron and a hammer. Finding a spot to fill, he pounded strands of a kind of rope called oakum into the narrow crack. Soaked in tar mixture, oakum helped to make the seams of the ship watertight. If water entered the ship at sea, the ship could sink. Openings around the trunnels were also filled. Men sealed these patches with tar, then scraped the hardened surfaces until they were smooth.

◀ *This diagram shows the decks of an 1850s American man-of-war.*

Shipbuilding in America

Shipbuilding was an important business in colonial America. Before 1776, most vessels were made for the British navy. Pine trees from New England's forests made choice **masts** for English ships. The colonists built smaller boats for fishing and for carrying people and goods among the colonies. In 1776, the **American Revolution** changed things. The colonies had no navy, so privately owned ships were armed with cannons and were sent to fight the British on the open seas. Some of these vessels sailed from Portsmouth's harbor.

America's first warships were built in New England's shipyards. ▶

John Langdon

Ben saw Mr. Langdon examining the *Ranger*'s hull. No doubt about it, John Langdon was a leading figure in Portsmouth. Born in 1741, he became a sea captain and then a successful merchant and shipbuilder. Now in his thirties, he was beginning a political career, as well.

In 1775, just before the American Revolution, Langdon had been elected as a representative to the second **Continental Congress**. He returned to Portsmouth with permission to build three warships. One of them was the *Ranger*.

◄ *John Langdon was a member of a respected family in New Hampshire.*

John Paul Jones

A short, well-dressed man entered the yard asking for John Langdon. Ben heard his Scottish accent and guessed he was probably John Paul Jones, the *Ranger*'s captain.

Ben knew that Jones was a fearless seaman. Word had it that he planned to attack the British Royal Navy in its own waters. British vessels were the finest in the world. The *Ranger* was only a modest, 18-gun warship.

Today, however, it would be tested for its ability to stand the challenges of battle and of the sea. Ben could hardly wait.

Today John Paul Jones is called the Father of the United States Navy. ▶

The Launch

Launching a ship was tricky business. A huge cradle supported the ship as it moved from the mold loft to the water. Tracks were greased to make the pathway smooth.

Ben joined the men who stood beside the series of stakes that steadied the ship. At a given signal, each man lifted his hammer and struck a wedge. The ship lifted just enough for workers to pull away the rear blocks. Slowly the ship inched toward the sea. When the final wedge was removed, the vessel slid safely into the water. Ben breathed a sigh of relief.

◀ *The* Ranger *and the* Drake *battle at sea.*

The Finishing Touches

Ben whistled happily as he crossed the bridge at the day's end. He knew that months of work lay ahead before the *Ranger* would be ready to sail. Tomorrow he would start work inside the ship. Three huge masts, with sails and rigging for support, had to be fitted. The ship was to be painted black with yellow trim. Ben also knew that when the *Ranger* left port under the command of Captain John Paul Jones, it would be the first ship to fly the new American flag. This was one day that Benjamin Tuthill would never forget.

Glossary

American Revolution (uh-MER-uh-ken reh-vuh-LOO-shun) Battles the American colonies fought against England for freedom.

apprenticeship (uh-PREN-tis-ship) The process by which an inexperienced person learns a skill or a trade.

bow (BOW) The forward part of a ship.

caulkers (KAH-kerz) Craftsmen who filled up the cracks or the seams of a ship to make it waterproof.

Continental Congress (kon-tin-EN-tul KON-gres) The delegates from each colony who declared America independent.

hull (HUL) The frame, or body, of a ship.

keel (KEEL) The long piece of wood at the bottom of a ship that runs from the front of the ship to the back.

launching (LONCH-ing) Setting a ship into water for the first time.

masts (MASTS) Long poles that rise from the deck of a ship. They support the ship's sails and rigging.

ribs (RIBZ) Parts of a ship's frame that run from the keel to the deck.

scale model (SKAYL MAH-duhl) An exact, though smaller, version of something.

sloop of war (SLOOP UV WOR) A small warship with guns only on one deck.

Index

Primary Sources

Cover: John Langdon. By James Sharples (1796–97). Independence National Historical Park. **(Cover Inset):** *The Aston Hall on the Thames*, a painting of a colonial sailing ship from The Mariners' Museum, Newport News, Virginia. By Francis Holman (1777). **Page 4:** *A Colonial Shipyard, circa 1768*. By Harold M. Hahn. The Mariners' Museum. **Page 7:** A New England shipyard. Hand–colored woodcut. *Harper's Monthly* (1878). **Page 8:** Hand colored woodcut of a boat being built. *Harper's Monthly* (1878). **Page 11:** Engraving of a shipwright from *The Book of Trades, or Library of Useful Arts*. Part I (1804). **Page 12:** Diagram of an American man-of-war ship. *Gleason's Pictorial Newspaper* (1854). **Page 15:** Hand-colored woodcut of colonial shipbuilding. *Old Times in the Colonies* By Coffin (1880). **Page 16:** John Langdon (See cover) **Page 19:** Portrait of John Paul Jones. By J. B. Longacre, after C. W. Peale (circa 1780). **Page 20:** Hand-colored engraving of the *Drake* and the *Ranger* at battle. By Carlton T. Chapman (1890).

Web Sites

Due to the changing nature of Internet links, PowerKids Press has developed an online list of Web sites related to the subject of this book. This site is updated regularly. Please use this link to access the list:
www.powerkidslinks.com/llwct/dlcship/